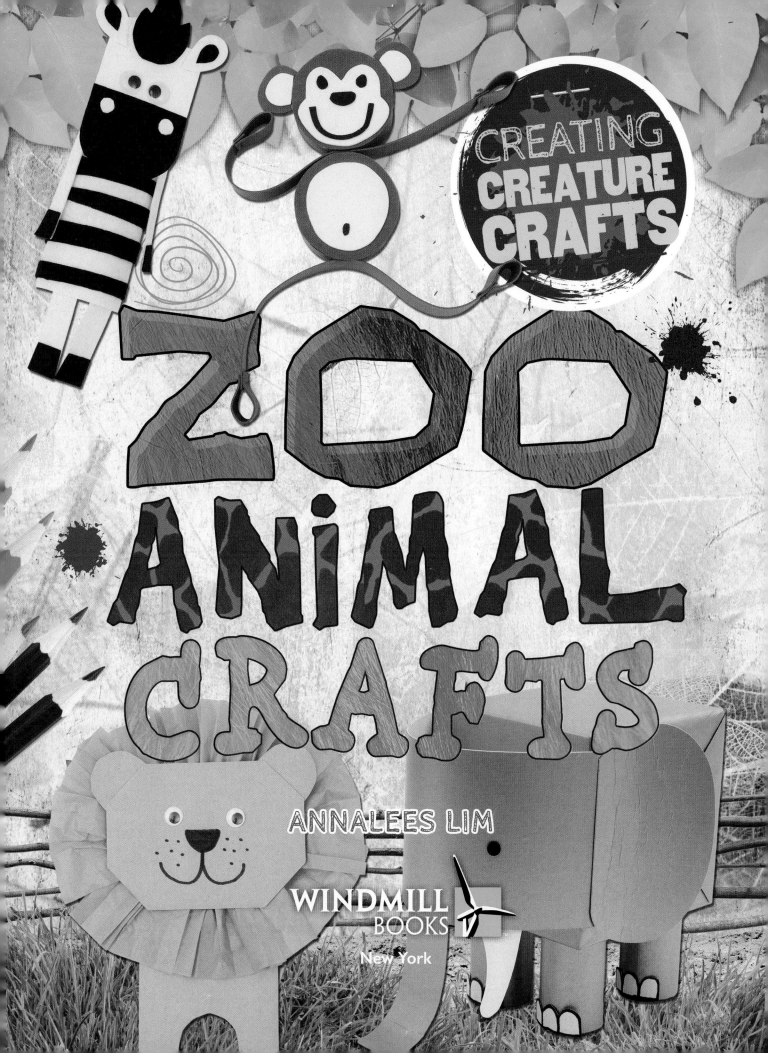

ZOO ANIMAL CRAFTS

CREATING CREATURE CRAFTS

ANNALEES LIM

WINDMILL
BOOKS
New York

CONTENTS

Welcome to the world of Zoo Animals

Zoos are great places to discover new animals that you have never seen before. The next time you take a trip to the zoo, see if you can spot all of the animals that are in this book. In the meantime, this book will show you how to make them and tell you lots of fun facts about them, too!

Some of the projects use paint and craft glue. When using these, always cover surfaces with a piece of plastic or layers of old newspaper. Whenever you can, let the project dry before moving on to the next step. This keeps things from getting stuck to each other and paint from smudging.

A note about measurements

Measurements are given in U.S. form with metric in parentheses. The metric conversion is rounded to make it easier to measure.

So, do you have your craft tools ready to go? Then get set to make your crafty creatures and discover what makes each of them so special!

LOOKOUT MEERKAT

In the wild, meerkats live in parts of southern Africa. You will often see lookout meerkats standing on their hind legs, keeping an eye out for any danger.

You will need:
Yogurt drink bottle
Brown paper bag
Brown paper
Card stock, 8½ by 11 inches (21.5 x 28cm)
Glue stick
Googly eyes
Pencil
Double-sided tape
Adhesive tape
Scissors
Brown felt-tipped pen

1

Cover the yogurt drink bottle in strips of double-sided tape. Peel off the back of the tape and stick on the brown paper bag.

2

Glue some brown paper onto the card stock.

4

3

Fold the paper-covered card stock in half and draw on a head, making sure that the nose touches the folded edge. Cut out the head and open it up.

4

Draw 2 arms, 2 legs and a tail onto the paper-covered card stock and cut them out.

5

Stick the arms, legs and tail to the bottle. Glue the googly eyes to the face and draw on the details with the brown felt-tipped pen. Use adhesive tape to fix the head to the bottle.

MEERKAT FACT

Young meerkats often help look after their newborn brothers and sisters.

TISSUE BOX ELEPHANT

Elephants are the largest animals that live on land. They can weigh over 15,000 pounds (7,000 kg) – that's about as much as four cars!

1

Wrap the tissue box neatly with gray paper, sticking it down with adhesive tape.

2

Cut the 2 rolls in half and cover all 4 pieces in gray paper. Stick all the rolls to the bottom of the box with adhesive tape.

3

Cut out a rectangle of gray card stock and curve it around the front of the box to make the head. Fix it to the box with sticky tape.

4

Cut out some ears, a trunk and a tail from gray card stock. Stick all of them to your elephant.

5

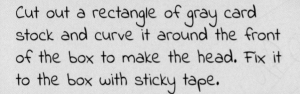

Draw 2 tusks and 4 sets of toes onto white paper. Cut them all out and stick them to your elephant. Draw on the eyes with the black marker.

ELEPHANT FACT

Did you know that elephants can swim very well? They use their trunk like a snorkel, so they can breathe when they are underwater!

EGG CARTON CAMEL

Camels live in places with hot weather. They have one or two bulges on their backs, called humps. This crafty camel's hump is made out of an egg carton!

You will need:
Egg carton
Yellow pipe cleaners
Yellow pom-pom
Yellow crêpe paper
Adhesive tape
Scissors
Black card stock
Googly eyes
Craft glue

1

Cover an egg carton section with yellow crêpe paper. Tuck any excess crêpe paper inside the egg carton section. Use tape to hold it in place.

2

Cut 2 pipe cleaners in half. Stick the 4 pieces inside the egg carton section to form the legs. Bend each of the ends to make the feet. This should make your camel stand on its own.

3

Bend the end of a pipe cleaner to form two ears. Stick the pipe cleaner to the front of the camel, using tape.

4

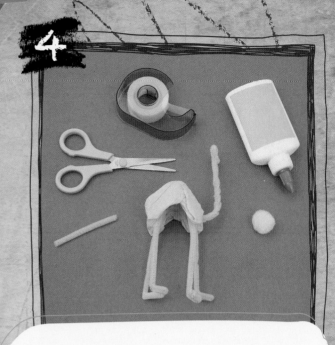

Make a tail out of a small section of pipe cleaner. Stick it to the back of the camel. Stick the pom-pom to the pipe cleaner that forms the neck and ears.

5

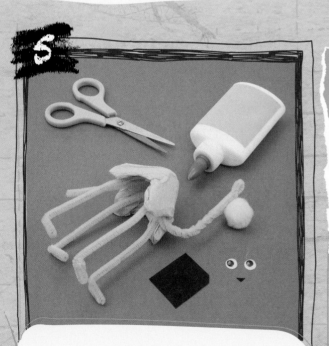

Glue googly eyes on the pom-pom. Cut out a small triangle of black card stock to make the nose and glue it to the pom-pom as well.

CAMEL FACT

People who live in the desert often ride camels. They also use camel milk for food.

FOAM MONKEY

Monkeys often live in woodland areas. They are very good climbers, and use their arms, legs and tail to swing from tree to tree.

You will need:
Brown, black and white foam
Craft glue
Stapler
Scissors

1

Cut brown foam into 4 strips that are the same size. Staple 2 into rings and staple one strip to each ring.

2

Staple both rings with their strips together, so that the rings form an "8."

3

Cut out 4 short strips of brown foam. Bend each of them to form a loop and staple them to the ends of the long strips.

4

Cut out 2 brown foam circles that are big enough to cover the rings. Cut out 2 small circles and stick them to one of the larger circles. Stick the larger circles to the rings.

5

Use white foam to make your monkey's face, inner ears and belly. Use black foam to make 2 eyes, a nose, a mouth and a belly button. Glue these all in place.

MONKEY FACT

Monkeys are our closest living relatives! They have hands that look like ours, with thumbs that help them to grip, eat food and groom.

STRIPY ZEBRA

Zebras are covered in black and white stripes. Each zebra has a stripy pattern that is one of a kind. You can make your zebra's pattern unique, too!

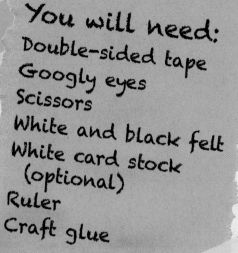

You will need:
Double-sided tape
Googly eyes
Scissors
White and black felt
White card stock (optional)
Ruler
Craft glue

1

Cut out a piece of white felt that is about 6 by 8 inches (15 x 20cm). Stick at least 3 strips of double-sided tape onto the black felt. Cut into thin strips and stick these to your white felt.

2

Roll your striped felt into a tube and stick the edges together using double-sided tape. If your felt is not thick enough to hold its shape, stick it to some white card stock first.

3

Use the white and black felt to make a zebra head and legs, with hooves.

4

Glue all of the felt pieces together. Stick them to the body of your zebra using double-sided tape.

5

Stick googly eyes onto your zebra's face.

ZEBRA FACT

Did you know that zebras don't lie down to sleep? They snooze while they are standing!

TISSUE PAPER LION

You can tell a male lion from a female one because males have large manes. Make your lion have a big, bushy mane using lots of tissue paper.

1

Fold the corners of one of the envelopes inwards. This will form your lion's face. Cut a small semicircle out of a short side of the other envelope.

2

Fold open the semicircle and cut it along the fold. Use the 2 semicircles to make your lion's ears. Stick them to either side of its head.

3

Cut rectangles out of the orange tissue. Fold them like an accordian. Stick them around the back of the folded envelope. Pull the ends apart to form the mane.

4

Draw the details of the face on using the black felt-tipped pen.

LION FACT

Lions live in groups of 10-15 animals. These groups are called prides.

5

Stick the head and body of your lion together using the glue stick. Glue on googly eyes.

STRAW FLAMINGO

Flamingos are large, pink birds that often stand on just one leg. Make your straw flamingo so that it balances on one leg, too!

You will need:
Pink bendy drinking straws
Pink tissue paper
Pink, black and orange paper
Scissors
Glue stick
Adhesive tape
Ruler
Googly eye

1

Trim 2 straws so that there is the same amount of straw on either side of their bendy parts. Insert one straw inside the other. This will form your flamingo's bent leg.

2

Bend the short part of a different straw to form the straight leg. Take another straw and cut it 2³/₈ inches (6cm) above the bend. Bend this too, to form your flamingo's neck.

3

Cut out a body shape and head shape from the pink paper. Stick the straws forming the legs to the body shape. Stick the straw forming the neck to the head shape.

4

Stick the body parts together. Cut out a beak shape from black paper and glue it to the head, along with a googly eye.

5

Cut out a circle of tissue paper and fold it like an accordion. This will form the wing. Stick this to your flamingo, along with some feet made from orange paper.

FLAMINGO FACT

Did you know that flamingos are so pink because of the food they eat? When they eat different food, they turn almost white!

PRINTED PAPER LEMUR

Most of the world's lemurs live on an island by Africa, called Madagascar. You can have fun making your own ring-tailed lemur by printing with a sponge!

You will need:
White card stock, 8½ by 11 inches (21.5 x 28cm)
Sponge
Black and gray paint
Black and yellow paper
Glue stick
Scissors
Black felt-tipped pen
Paint palette

1 Use the sponge to color half of your white card stock gray. Only press the sponge down lightly, so that you create a patchy pattern.

2 Clean the sponge and use it to paint some black stripes onto the other half of your card stock. Leave the bottom third of this section white. Leave the card stock to dry.

3

On the gray side, use the black felt-tipped pen to draw the body, arms and legs of your lemur.

4

On the other side, draw a curly tail on the striped part and a head on the white part. Cut out all the shapes.

5

Cut out pieces from the gray side to form the top of the head and the tufts. Cut out 2 patches and a nose from black paper, and 2 eyes from yellow paper. Glue all the pieces together. Draw on the pupils with the black felt-tipped pen.

LEMUR FACT

Lemurs love to be in the sun! They enjoy sitting in the sunshine, sometimes for whole afternoons.

PAPER PLATE SEA LION

Sea lions spend a lot of time in the water and are great swimmers. They can hold their breath for at least 10 minutes when they are underwater!

You will need:
3 paper plates
Blue, pink and purple paint
Black card stock
Googly eye
Scissors
Paintbrush
Glue stick
Black felt-tipped pen
Paint palette

1

Paint 3 paper plates, one in blue, one in purple and one in pink. Let them dry.

2

Cut a curved shape out of the pink plate and stick it to the blue plate. This will form a rock for your sea lion.

3

Draw a sea lion body, fin and tail onto the purple plate. Cut out all the shapes.

4

Cut out a nose from a piece of black card stock. Stick this onto the head, along with a googly eye.

5

Glue all the pieces together onto the blue plate.

SEA LION FACT

Male sea lions are called bulls, females are called cows and baby sea lions are called pups.

PLASTIC POT TIGER

You will need:
Orange card stock
Black electrical tape
Large yogurt cup
Scissors
Googly eyes
Glue stick
Black felt-tipped pen
Adhesive tape

Tigers have orange coats with black stripes. Like the stripy pattern on a zebra, each tiger's coat is unique. Your tiger can have its very own special stripes!

1

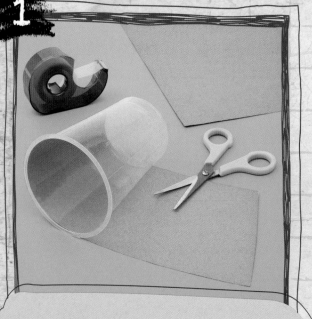

Cover the yogurt cup with orange card stock. If your cup has a label, you can remove it and use it as a template for the orange card stock.

2

Cut strips of black tape into triangles and stick them onto the side of the cup. These are your tiger's stripes.

22

3

Make 2 ears out of orange card stock. Stick them to the top of the cup.

4

Add the inside of the ears, a nose and a mouth. You can use either electrical tape or a black felt-tipped pen for this. Use the glue stick to add googly eyes.

5

Tape some thin black stripes onto a piece of orange card stock and cut out 4 legs. Stick these to your tiger's body.

TIGER FACT

Did you know that tigers are great swimmers? They go for a dip to cool off when the weather is hot.

GLOSSARY

coat — an animal's fur
groom — when an animal cleans its own or another animal's fur
hind legs — an animal's back legs
mane — long hair around a male lion's face
template — a shape that is used as a guide to cut out something
trunk — the nose of an elephant; it is long and shaped a bit like a hose
unique — when something is one of a kind, not like anything else

INDEX

Published in 2015 by Windmill Books,
an Imprint of Rosen Publishing
29 East 21st Street, New York, NY 10010

Copyright © 2016 Wayland/Windmill

Series editor: Julia Adams
Craft photography: Simon Pask, N1 Studios
Additional images: Shutterstock

Cataloging-in-Publication Data

Lim, Annalees.
Zoo animal crafts / by Annalees Lim.
p. cm. — (Creating creature crafts)
Includes index.
ISBN 978-1-5081-9121-6 (pbk.)
ISBN 978-1-5081-9122-3 (6-pack)
ISBN 978-1-5081-9123-0 (library binding)
1. Handicraft – Juvenile literature. 2. Zoo animals
– Juvenile literature. 3. Animals in art – Juvenile
literature.
I. Lim, Annalees. II. Title.
TT160.L56 2016
743'.6-d23

Manufactured in the United States of America
CPSIA Compliance Information: Batch #BW16PK. For Further Information contact
Rosen Publishing, New York, New York at 1-800-237-9932.